The Solitary Christian Mysticism Manual

Magic Quest, Volume 5

Gideon Crusader

Published by Gideon Crusader, 2022.

While every precaution has been taken in the preparation of this book, the publisher assumes no responsibility for errors or omissions, or for damages resulting from the use of the information contained herein.

THE SOLITARY CHRISTIAN MYSTICISM MANUAL

First edition. November 21, 2022.

ISBN: 979-8215821206

Written by Gideon Crusader.

Also by Gideon Crusader

Magic Quest
A Codex on Creating a Magical Phantom
Prosperity Magic for Money & Wealth
Telekinesis Bible
Beware of the Modern World
The Solitary Christian Mysticism Manual

Standalone
Frugal Living for Happiness & Freedom

Table of Contents

For J.

Introduction

Magic Quest: The Solitary Christian Mysticism Manual reveals the path that you can take to practice Christian mysticism on your own and in the comfort of your home. Indeed, so many witches, wizards, and magical practitioners are now turning to Christ for a deeper and genuine spirituality. Now is your chance to join in this beautiful, magical, and divine universe. The way to Christ is the way of the heart and soul. And, yes, this is something that you can do right now, and it is something that can change your life forever.

It is strongly suggested that you forget about everything that you think you know about Jesus Christ and Christianity. We are going to start from scratch, with a clean and undefiled slate. If you are wondering why the book teaches following Christ in a solitary way, the reason for this is that Jesus Christ is for all people, regardless of race and religion, and regardless of their personal circumstances in life. Christ is for all. And, yes, you can follow the Divine Master, Jesus Christ, on your own, even without being a member of any formal religious group. Christ is for all. Not to mention there are also many people these days who are discouraged because of the evils being done by their religion. It should be clarified that there is a big difference between religion and the real Jesus Christ. There is also a big difference between those who believe in Christ and those who actually and sincerely follow in the footsteps of the Divine Master.

Magic Quest: The Solitary Christian Mysticism Manual is written in an easy-to-understand format, so that you can conveniently focus only on learning and applying all the teachings into your life. Anyone has the golden opportunity to follow Christ. Whether you are loyal to your religion or not, you can follow Christ, and this is something that you can do right now.

What about mysticism? Many people get intimidated when they encounter the term, *mysticism*, but that should not really be the case. In fact, some people say that we are all called to be a mystic. Mysticism is simply having a spiritual union with Christ. It is where we elevate our soul and unite it with the Divine. To me, this is a very profound way and an experience of Christ in our life. From this standpoint, indeed, we are called to be a mystic, for every creature must surrender to its Creator.

Are you ready for a magical and spiritual adventure? Are you ready to elevate your soul and taste the presence of the Divine Master, Jesus Christ? If yes, then let me now welcome you into this world. Come, take a leap of faith, and you shall dance among the tremulous stars.

What is Solitary Christian Mysticism?

Christian mysticism has been in existence for centuries. It is the practice of following Jesus Christ and having a union with Him. The term *Christian* simply refers to someone who follows Jesus Christ. The term *mysticism* is simply a spiritual practice of having a union with the Divine. It is where the soul is elevated to taste the Divine Presence. It is oneness with God.

What about being solitary? This simply means that you are approaching and following Christ on your own. This does not need to be understood in a strict way. You can still follow the teachings in this book even if you are loyal to your religion or whatever group of friends that you have.

We have to understand that Christ is for all people. When Christ suffered and died, He did not just do it for the righteous and the holy. In fact, Christ came mainly for sinners, and the salvation that He offers is for all, without any discrimination and preference.

Now, there are people who seem to get intimidated when they encounter the term *Solitary Christian Mysticism* and the likes. However, it should be clarified that solitary Christian mysticism is actually very easy and simple as long as you know how to do it properly. Another good news is that there are really no hard and fast rules or any formality that you should observe to do it well. Think of it as developing an intimate relationship with Jesus. It is just like having a relationship with someone much like a profound friendship; but this time, you are building this relationship with Christ.

It is up to you whether having a relationship is enough, but you also have the option to pursue the practice of mysticism. Mysticism simply makes things much more intimate and genuine. It is a taste of Christ, a direct experience of His presence in your life—a union of your soul with the Divine. It is a mysterious experience, and it is simply wonderful. There are a good number of mystics in history, such as St. John the Baptist, St. Francis, St. Padre Pio, St. Catherine, St. Faustina, Crowley, Gautama Buddha, Heinrich Agrippa, and even Confucius may be considered a mystic, among many others. You may notice that some of the people that I have just mentioned were not Christians. This is because mysticism is not limited in scope to Christianity. After all, divine spiritual energy is not limited to any religion and traditional beliefs. It encompasses all and pervades us.

What about you, what makes you interested in solitary Christian mysticism? I am glad that you are learning this path. Many magical practitioners are also turning to Christ these days for a deep and genuine spirituality, and I hope that you may also find what you are seeking in Christ. I am sure that you will as long as you approach Christ with humility and sincerity.

Humility is Important

When we approach Christ or if we do anything that is spiritual, it is important for us to be humble. Being humble allows the grace of God to flow in and through us. There is an interesting story in Buddhism about the importance of humility, and it goes something like this:

A novice monk went to a master monk. He wanted the master monk to take him as a disciple. As soon as he met the master monk, he did all his best to impress him (the master monk) by telling him everything that he knew about spirituality. He was so proud of all his knowledge and boasted about it. The master monk kept his silence and did not even look interested in whatever the novice monk was saying. As soon as the novice monk finished talking, the master monk poured his tea into a cup. He continued to do so even though it was already full and overflowing. The sight of the tea continuously spilling from the cup made the novice monk feel very uncomfortable, so he called the master monk's attention to it. But, the master monk did not mind it and continued to pour tea into the already overflowing cup. He then stopped pouring tea, looked at the novice monk, and smiled at him. *Do you see what has just happened here?* asked the master monk. The novice monk said no. To which the master monk explained, *Just like this cup that is so full of itself and could not accept new tea, so is your mind so full of itself and could not accept new teachings. If you really want to learn and be my disciple, you must first empty your cup. Be humble. Empty your mind, so that it will be able to receive new teachings and wisdom. At that* point, the novice monk apologized and humbled himself, and then the master monk took him as his disciple.

The same is true when we follow Christ. We should also be humble. This also reminds me of the teaching of Christ which says that whoever exalts himself will be humbled, and he who humbles himself will be exalted. In the said story, the novice monk exalted himself, and he was embarrassed. It was only when he humbled himself when he finally understood and gained wisdom, and only after that did the master monk take him as his disciple.

But what does it really mean to be humble? To be humble is to empty one's self. Just as you have to empty a cup for it to be filled with new tea, so should you empty yourself so that divine energy can enter and fill you. How can Christ fill you when you are so full of yourself? Therefore, let us always be humble, so that we may always receive the graces of the Almighty.

The Importance of Meditation

The practice of meditation is a good way to be humble. In fact, real meditation is a humbling experience. Now, do not let this discourage you. Doing meditation is actually very easy and simple. In fact, it is more about not doing anything rather than requiring you to do something. Meditation clears and empties the mind. In fact, in many occult circles, it is encouraged to begin any magical work with meditation. Even a few minutes of meditation can help greatly.

The early Christians, especially the so-called Desert Fathers and Mothers of Egypt, also practiced meditation. Sadly, in our modern time, only a few Christians know and practice meditation. You do not need to be like the majority of believers these days for you can always practice meditation on your own, at any time and as often as you want, and even in the comfort of your home.

But what is meditation? For some people, it is a way of relaxing the mind; but to others, it means so much more than that. Here is the answer: meditation is what you make it. If you just think that it is a way to relax the mind and destress, then so be it. However, it should be emphasized that true meditation is, first and foremost, a spiritual practice. It was practiced by many leading figures from various religions; and as such, it is not exclusive to any single religion. Meditation is for all, even for those who do not believe in God or in any form of spirituality.

The best way to know meditation is through actual experience. The meditation technique that you are about to learn is a basic breathing meditation, which is probably the simplest meditation technique in the world, but it is also one of the most powerful and effective techniques. In fact, its power lies in its simplicity. Many advanced meditators also stick to just practicing this meditation alone in exclusion of all the others. As you can see, this is a really good meditation. It has a direct and simple approach. Having said that, the steps are as follows:

Assume a comfortable position and relax. Close your eyes, and do not think about anything. Clear your mind. Now, breathe gently through your nose. Gently focus on your breath. If thoughts arise in the mind (which they usually do) or if you find yourself wandering away from the breath, simply bring your attention back to your breath. Just relax and stay calm, and do not use any kind of force. Meditation is a moment of stillness and peace. Just relax, focus on your breath, and let go.

Nothing must exist in your mind but the breath. Be one with your breath. If thoughts come like a river, just let them pass like the waters of a river. Stay calm and relaxed at all times. Surrender to the breath. Breath is life, and he who meditates on the breath meditates on life. Be one with the breath. Be the breath. Become life.

At any time that you want to end this meditation, simply bring your awareness back to your physical body, move your fingers and toes, and then very gently open your eyes with a smile.

As a basic rule in magic and mysticism, one should meditate at least twice daily. If you can do more, then that would be better. Now, the length of time that you meditate does not matter that much because once you reach a deep state of mind and being, time simply ceases to exist. This actually explains how many advanced meditators and masters are able to sit in meditation for very long hours without getting bothered or distracted. With enough and regular practice, you can also achieve this mindset and level of consciousness.

It is the emptying and surrender of the mind that accompanies this meditation which makes it really powerful. It is not uncommon for even those who are trying this meditation for the first time to experience a profound state of mind that is full of peace and harmony. Nevertheless, if you do not feel anything after several attempts, do not be discouraged. Just keep on practicing, and you will surely attain positive results very soon.

Whether or not you believe in God, you can safely practice this meditation and enjoy its physical, mental, emotional, and spiritual benefits. This meditation only concerns the breath, so you do not need to be alarmed by anything. Just be open, relax, and breathe—and the magic of the universe shall unfold right before you.

Know Jesus Christ

Before you make the conscious effort to follow Christ, you must first get to know who He is; and fortunately, this is very easy to do. An excellent first step is to read the Bible. Now, do not be discouraged; I know that the Bible can look intimidating because it is very thick. However, you do not really need to read the whole book in one sitting. You see, the Bible is a library. It is composed of many books. It has two main divisions: the Old Testament and the New Testament.

If you are just starting out and you would like to get to know Christ, then it is strongly suggested that you start by reading the Bible, specifically the Book of Matthew, which also happens to be the very first book in the New Testament. By reading the said book, you will learn about the life and divine teachings of the Divine Master, Jesus Christ. It is not a long book. In fact, I was able to finish reading it in one sitting.

After reading the Book of Matthew, and if you feel like you would like to learn more about Christ, then feel free to read the other books, such as the books of John, Mark, and Luke. All these four books (Matthew, Mark, Luke, and John) are similar books in the sense that they talk about the life and teachings of Jesus Christ. They are not completely the same. In fact, there are some stories and teachings that are found in one book but not in the other books, so it is strongly recommended that you read all of them. Of course, you are always free to read all the other books of the Bible, even those in the Old Testament.

It also helps to know and learn from those people who have come before you, such as the saints. By reading the lives of the saints, you can have a clearer picture of who Jesus is and what may happen when you follow Him.

Now, knowing Christ is one thing, following Him is another. But, why would anyone want to follow Christ? This leads us to our next topic.

Why Follow Christ?

So, why should we follow Christ? Truth be told, Jesus Christ is the one and true God. I know that there are many other gods out there who are claiming to be a god, so why follow Christ and not them? Unlike other gods, Christ loves you. He suffered and died for you. Also, unlike other gods that will require you to conduct a formal ritual just to be able to call on them, Christ does not require any of these things, for He is already with you because He is God. You can just call on His name at any time, and rest assured that He always hears for He is always with you.

Jesus also took human form and lived a completely human life. Therefore, you can rest assured that He understands what you are going through as a human being. And, more importantly, He is the God who loves you, and even suffered and died for you, so that you may be saved and enjoy eternal life.

For a long time, people wondered what God was like. How did He look and what are His thoughts concerning humans? Jesus came and made all these questions clear to everyone. Indeed, He is the Divine Master, the Way, the Truth, and the Eternal Life.

Now, following Christ does not require of us anything. No matter where we may stand in life, regardless of our personal circumstances, we can be sure that we can follow Him. Based on the written accounts in the scriptures (the Bible), it can be seen that Jesus does not even look at your past, for He is with you even if you think that you are the vilest human in the world. In fact, Jesus made friends with sinners, and He saved them. He showed them a better way to live. He taught Him His way, which is the way of God.

Nevertheless, Christ does not force anyone to follow Him. It is up to you to make a choice. I would suggest that you try to do so, for it might just be the greatest journey that you could take in your life. Do not worry, you can always turn around and walk away if you ever feel like it is not for you, but at least give it a try. You deserve to be given this chance—a divine encounter with Christ, the God of Love, and the One, True, Living God.

How to Follow Christ

How exactly do we follow Christ? Fortunately, there are no hard and fast rules on this matter, but the important thing is to abide by His teachings. Now, to know the teachings of the Master, we just have to read the Bible. Again, you do not need to read the whole Bible, but just the parts about Jesus' life and teachings would be enough. Still, you are free to read the other books and learn from them. I strongly suggest reading the Book of Psalms as well.

Once you become a true follower of Christ, Jesus will even manifest Himself to you and make Himself known to you. Jesus Himself said so in the scriptures. Of course, how He is going to do that would be up to Him. But, rest assured that you will soon have a real and intimate relationship with God, Jesus Christ.

For starters, it is good to just focus on reading the life and teachings of Christ. Again, I strongly recommend that you start by reading the Book of Matthew. You can follow it up with the Book of John, Luke, and Mark. It does not have to be in proper order. Pay attention to the life and divine teachings of Christ.

So, just to summarize, first we humble ourselves, and then we practice meditation to help us have the right state of mind. Once the mind is ready, we can then read the story of Christ and His teachings in the Bible. It does not really have to be this formal. In fact, I know someone who ended up following Christ simply by reading the Book of Matthew alone. It grabbed his interest, and He simply pursued Christ right there and then.

There is no right or wrong way to do it as long as the heart is sincere. In fact, Jesus will even help you do it. Just say His name and ask for His help. Rest assured that He is always with you.

Reading the Bible would be really helpful. It would be an excellent step that you can do very easily on your own.

How to Read the Bible

Let us now talk about reading the Bible. How do you read the Bible? Is there a right or wrong way to read it? There are two main ways of reading the Bible: the Antiochian method and the Alexandrian method. The Antiochian method is the most common way of reading the Bible. It is how most people read and understand the Bible. If you are reading the Bible for the first time, then this method of reading is recommended. According to the Antiochian method, the Bible is to be understood by the meaning of the words that the texts convey. This is where you interpret the Bible based solely on the texts that are written. Simply put, it is based on the written words and nothing more. It takes the words in the Bible literally. It is just like you are reading a newspaper or a novel. This is a good method, and many people are satisfied with sticking to this method. For many people, this approach of reading the Bible is enough for them, and there might be nothing wrong with that.

However, in mysticism, we learn another method of reading the Bible, and that is the Alexandrian method. This reading approach gives a whole new meaning and depth to the reading of the sacred scriptures. Under this method, you do not take the words by their literal meaning. But rather, you take the Bible as a metaphor where the words and names and stories act as symbols. For example, in reading the famous story of David and Goliath, you may view Goliath as the biggest problem that you are currently facing in life, and then you are David. Know that no matter how big your problem may be and how hopeless you might be to overcome it, you can overcome all problems and challenges with the help of God, and so there is nothing at all that you should fear.

As a Christian mystic, you should learn both methods of reading the Bible. When reading the Bible or any stories therein for the first few times, it is recommended to apply the Antiochian method. Once you gain more familiarity with the story, then you can deepen your experience of the scriptures by using the Alexandrian method.

Unlike the Antiochian method which interprets the Bible literally, the Alexandrian method opens a whole new world for you. The important thing here is to keep your mind open, as well as your imagination.

If you apply the Alexandrian method properly, and if you practice it regularly, then you will surely have a mystifying encounter and experience of the scriptures. It turns a mere reading of what is a mere historical record/account into a personal experience of the Divine. This converts the reading of the scriptures into a solemn meditation.

The Alexandrian method usually takes practice. Nevertheless, it is a learnable skill, and you will naturally get good at it the more that you practice it. You can apply your present situation to your readings and allow the scripture to guide you. It is also recommended that you pray to Jesus whenever you use this method, so that He could guide you deeper into the mystery.

Imaginative Prayer

Since we discussed the Alexandrian method, you should also learn about the so-called *imaginative prayer* or the art of praying with the imagination. This was made popular by St. Ignatius, but it should be noted that this form of prayer has long been in existence even before his time. Still, thanks to him, this technique has drawn more attention and interest.

So what is imaginative prayer? Imaginative prayer is where you allow the imagination to take full reign in your prayer. It comes from the foundation and realization that God is the God of all; and as such, He is also the God of the imagination. The best way to understand imaginative prayer is through actual practice. Here are the steps:

Choose a particular story in the Bible. Any story will do. If you are just starting out, simply pick a scene in the story of Jesus. Now, read this particular story a few times to gain more familiarity with it. Next, close your eyes and imagine the story unfolding right in front of you. However, do not just imagine it visually, but see and feel that you are within the story. For example, let us say that you are imagining the scene where Christ tells Peter to walk on the water with Him. See and feel that you are on the boat together with the other disciples. See and feel the strong winds and the boat moving about due to the storm. Look at Christ standing on the water. Be active within the imaginary scene. In fact, if you want, you can imagine yourself as St. Peter, and Jesus is telling you to come to Him and walk on the water. The key here is to use your imagination to the fullest, allowing you to experience the story. In your imagination, it is no longer the story of the past, but it is unfolding right now at this very moment, and you are an active part of it.

Do not hesitate to apply your imagination to its fullest extent. Use as many senses as you are comfortable with while you are immersed in your imaginary world of the sacred scriptures. It may happen that the story may not unfold in the same way as you have read it. This is normal and okay, so do not try to control anything. Just let the story flow naturally on its own, and just relax and be open. Enjoy every moment of the journey, and rest assured that every step that you take is with God. After all, God is the God of All, including the God of the imagination.

Self-Renunciation

Christ said that whoever wants to come after Him must deny themselves, take up their cross, and follow Him. This is similar to the teaching of emptying one's cup, so that you can welcome new tea into your cup. After learning about the teachings of Christ, the next step is putting them into practice. This is called living the teachings, and this is what it means to be a true follower of Christ.

It is very easy to follow Christ when things are going well and easy. However, what happens when things are not working out the way that you want them to? Or, how about when the power of temptation gets too strong for you to handle? When we follow Christ, we must also renounce ourselves. Now, it should be clarified that this self-renunciation is actually what is good for us. It is not a sacrifice that will benefit the Lord, but it is actually for our own benefit.

Which do you think is better: the version of yourself that is designed by your own limited mind or the version of yourself that is in accordance with the design of the Infinite Mind? If you want to discover the real and full beauty of the soul, then we must work with God and follow His divine teachings.

When there is a clash between your own will and the will of God, we must be ready to let go of our own will to make way for the realization and manifestation of the Divine Will, which is also what is best for us. Unfortunately, there are times when this is easier said than done. However, whenever you find yourself in this kind of situation, just remember the basics. Many times, the basic teachings of Christ will be more than enough to deal with the many challenges of life, including all of the temptations that go with it.

Do not let the term *self-renunciation* dishearten you. Think of it as a way to get rid of all the illusions in your life, so that you can discover and experience the real you. It is not about losing who you truly are, but it is more about finding who you really are. The *self* here is not your very essence, for the real you is holy and divine, made in the image and likeness of God. But rather, the *self* that will be lost is simply the *ego-self*. It is the *self* that prevents you from realizing who you truly are. By coming to Christ, we can free ourselves from the illusions of this world and enjoy real peace and freedom.

Have Faith

Having faith is not something that you can just pretend. It is either you have it or you do not have it at all. Faith also means so much more than just believing in something. After all, even the demons know and believe that Jesus Christ is God. According to scriptures, faith is the realization of the things that are hoped for and the evidence of things that we cannot see. Many holy people also say that with the power of faith, one can cast miracles and make wonders. It should be clarified that it is not really you who is making the miracles happen, but it is Christ working through you. You become a chosen vessel through which Christ works and casts His miracles. This faith is also not faith in one's self, but it is faith in the Living God, Jesus Christ.

Faith—and I mean real faith—is not something that just happens in a moment. But rather, it is something that you build over time. It is what blooms and grows when you have a deepening relationship with Christ. There are no secret formulas for this. It is just a matter of following Christ and having a closer relationship with Him. Soon enough, you will know Christ more than how people could know through mere reading the Bible, for Jesus Christ is as alive today as He was thousands of years ago. He loved you then, and He loves you even more now, always, and forever.

How is faith different from merely believing? There is a world of difference between the two. Even demons believe in Christ, and yet they do not have faith. Faith necessarily includes trust, and even complete reliance on God. This faith is also not something that can be made up, but it must be sincere and true. Through human efforts alone, it is impossible to have real faith, for real faith is only possible with the help of God.

For now, do not worry about building a very strong faith. You will come to it at the right time. After all, the best way to have faith and grow it is not by thinking about faith, but it is by learning more about Christ and following Him by obeying His teachings.

On Prayer

Prayer is commonly understood as a communication with God. However, many people seem to have an incomplete practice of faith where they are just the ones who are doing the talking all the time. We tend to forget that we also ought to listen. When it comes to listening to the voice of God, the practice of imaginative prayer and the Alexandrian method of reading the Bible will be of great help as they allow us to listen to Him. This does not mean that verbal prayer is not desirable, but just do not limit yourself to it.

There is a gift from God. It is so beautiful, and yet so many people take it for granted. Imagine having this gift where you always have access to the Divine. It is far beyond any modern communication technology. Indeed, we should make good use of prayer and take advantage of it as much as we can.

According to St. Paul, we should pray ceaselessly. We must remind ourselves that we are always in the presence of God because God is always with us. This is true even though at times we may not be aware of His divine presence.

It is also our responsibility to establish a good and healthy prayer life. In our modern world where so many people are always busy and stressed out with the matters of the world, it may be difficult to pray and to pray enough. We must learn to prioritize our spiritual life and to make time for prayer. Doing so usually involves a conscious and deliberate act to actually pray. Especially if you are just starting out, making time to pray regularly may be a challenge. But, do not lose heart. You should give yourself enough time to adjust. Soon enough, praying will be a natural thing for you, and even a need that you must do every day and night.

No matter how busy your life might be, make sure to have time to pray. In fact, the busier your life gets, the more that you need to pray. Praying is also an effective way to develop a deeper and closer relationship with Christ.

When you develop some spiritual maturity, you will realize that everything that you do actually depends on God. This only makes it more necessary for you to pray as often as you can. From now on, be sure to prioritize your prayer life, and remember that prayer is a gift that allows you to be connected to Christ all the time.

The Jesus Prayer

The *Jesus Prayer* is a beautiful prayer that is practiced by many spiritual seekers and monks. Those who pray it devoutly also report mystical experiences. Indeed, it is a prayer that you will find highly beneficial. In fact, some mystics do almost nothing else but to pray this prayer as much as they can. Indeed, this is something that is very much worth learning.

The Jesus Prayer has two versions. There is a short version and a long version. The long version is actually not long, but it just happens to be longer than the other version by just two words.

The Jesus prayer is simply this: *Lord Jesus Christ, Son of God, have mercy on me.* The longer version is this: *Lord Jesus Christ, Son of God, have mercy on me, a sinner.* You can use either version for they are equally effective, and one is not better than the other, so feel free to use whichever is more comfortable for you.

The Jesus Prayer is actually a form of meditation. You just have to say it and focus on it. You can use the exact steps for the breathing meditation that we have discussed; but instead of focusing on the breath, you repeatedly and lovingly say and focus on the Jesus Prayer.

It is strongly advised that you practice this meditative prayer as often as you can. It is a very powerful prayer and meditation. But you do not always have to pray the Jesus Prayer as a form of meditation. It can also be prayed casually, such as by saying it at any time even when you are engaged in any activity. It helps remind you of Christ and also brings you in communion with

Him at any time. You can say the prayer out loud, as a whisper, or even silently in your mind only. Indeed, there is so much that you can gain from reciting this prayer. So, give it a try and see how it works for you.

On Sin

Sin ruins the relationship that we have with God. It damages our soul. As a follower of Christ, we should not sin, and we should avoid all temptations to sin. Now, temptations will surely come. Even Christ was tempted by the devil in the desert. Temptation is not completely bad. Holy men and women said that temptations are necessary to achieve holiness. Think of temptations as the spiritual weights that we lift to strengthen our soul.

What exactly is sin? Sin is simply anything that is not in accordance with the will of God. There are sins that are very obvious, such as killing, stealing, and so on; but there is also a kind of sin that is less subtle. It is the kind that is not completely wrong in its face, but the only thing that makes it a sin is that it is not the will of God. This is another reason why we need to be closer to Christ, so that we can always know the will of God. The will of God is what is best for us. We can always trust and rely on His Infinite Mind and Wisdom.

Now, there is a difference between facing a temptation and falling into it. We ought not to fall into temptation because falling into temptation would mean committing a sin. If you walk the spiritual path, be ready to face a great number of temptations. Nevertheless, do not worry. Be of good courage because you can rest assured that with every temptation that you may face, you will not go through it alone because Christ is always with you.

There are many ways how a follower of Christ handles the matter of sin. There are those who beat themselves for being terrible sinners, but there are also those who have freed themselves from sin, so much so that they do not even think about it. A good story to read in this regard is the story of the woman caught in adultery. It is worth noting that in the said story, Christ did not condemn the woman. In fact, He even saved her from being stoned to death. He defended her. And, He also told her that He does not condemn her, and then He gently dismissed the issue of sin by simply telling her to go and sin no more. So great and wonderful is our Christ, indeed. It is suggested that you use this story for your imaginative prayer, and place yourself in the shoes of the woman caught in adultery. Her story can be found in John 8:1-11.

As for me, I prefer to rise above sin with the love of Jesus. According to a saint, our goal is not only not to sin but to rise spiritually. Not sinning alone is not enough. As true followers of Christ, we should not be afraid of sin for we are well above it. The love of Christ has saves us from the slavery of sin. We have passed from death to life because of Him.

Although we may do our best not to sin, we may find ourselves falling into it every now and then. When this happens, be sorry and learn from the experience. Know that Christ loves and heals you. Just do your best not to sin again.

On a positive note, sin teaches us to be humble. Every time that we sin, we can realize that we need to pray and be closer to Him.

Never allow yourself to be trapped in sin. Know very well and with certainty that Christ has freed you from sin, even from the effects of sin. Instead of living in sin (which can barely be called living at all), we must live in Christ.

Self-Annihilation

The experience of self-annihilation is not something to bother about if you are just a beginner. However, it is still good to be aware of it. This experience, which is also a challenge, happens in the higher level of the soul.

We have discussed self-renunciation. Self-annihilation is similar to it, but this one is of a higher level. Here, the ego is completely destroyed and not just simply renounced. There is the total loss of the sense of self. It is not just merely renouncing the self, but it is a complete destruction and annihilation of the self where it shall cease to exist.

Do not think of this as some kind of punishment. But rather, this is an important stage to transcend a higher level of spirituality. Do not worry, you will not enter this stage if your soul is not ready. This spiritual undertaking is only bestowed on those who are ready.

It should also be noted that during this time, you may feel as if Christ has abandoned you. But, do not fear because you can rest assured that He is always with you, even during those moments when you do not feel His presence. After all, real faith does not depend on what the senses can perceive. This is like your turn to experience what Christ experienced in the Garden of Gethsemane or when He was on the cross forsaken by everyone.

When you reach this level, you need to stay strong and not fear anything. Know that if you manage to go through this challenge and overcome it, there will be significant development in your soul. It is like the awakening of the giant within you. Indeed, this hardship is necessary for the soul to further evolve into great heights.

This self-annihilation is necessary for the True Self to blossom and grow. Many mystics have been through this experience. It is an important experience; and if you just stay strong and keep your faith in Christ, you will receive tremendous divine blessings in return.

On Divine Energy

In the occult and magical arts, there is this belief in magical energy, also known as *life force energy*. In mysticism, we also believe in the existence of the said energy, and we usually refer to it as *divine energy*. It does not really what you call it, but it is your understanding of it that matters.

So what is the nature of this divine energy? This divine energy pervades the whole universe. It is inside you and all around you. It is also eternal in the sense that it cannot be destroyed or killed. Yes, it does not die. As such, there are those who think of this divine energy as being God Himself. However, the majority school of thought is of the belief that this divine energy is not the completeness of God, but may only be considered as the energy of God—or at the most, the breath of Divinity.

Personally, I share the view that divine energy is not God per se. The reason for this is that this energy can be easily manipulated by the mind if you just know how to do it properly. In fact, there is a practice in occultism known as energy manipulation. To say that this divine energy is God in His absolute form is like saying that you can, with your mind, easily manipulate God. Needless to say, such an idea is really absurd.

This divine energy connects us to everything and everyone; hence, the saying, *We are one.* It is the energy that creates the so-called *web of life*.

Unlike the wizards and witches, Christian mystics no longer manipulate divine energy deliberately. Instead, we now allow the works and grace of God to direct everything that happens in our life.

In history, there are still those who attempted to control this divine energy and used it for good, such as for healing and/or for giving motivation. It is actually very easy, and it is good that you know about it just so you can have a better understanding of it. The best way to understand it is through actual practice. Here is a simple exercise that you can do:

For this exercise, you are going to use divine energy for healing. Assume a comfortable position and relax. Close your eyes and free your mind. Magical energy is all around you. Imagine this magical energy as pure white light everywhere. Since you are going to use it for healing, know that this magical energy is charged with powerful healing energy. It heals everything that it touches. Now, see and feel that you are drawing this magical energy toward you and pour it into yourself. Absorb the healing energy greedily like a sponge absorbing the water. Allow yourself to be filled with this powerful healing energy. Continue this for as long as you like. When you are done, slowly open your eyes as you return to ordinary consciousness. You can then go about your day knowing that your whole body and being are fully charged with healing energy.

It is worth reminding that the aforesaid practice is now rarely practiced by mystics since the primary approach these days is based on total renunciation to God. We no longer mess with the natural flow of divine energy. If we intend to make any changes to it, mystics usually resort to prayer and meditation. A common pitfall when one gets used to manipulating energy is that it tends to feed the ego, thereby making self-renunciation almost impossible. But, when one completely surrenders to God, it is all that is necessary for the Divine Master will never leave you. He loves you, and that is all that matters.

The Devil

Who is the devil? There are various literatures on this subject. The devil simply means an adversary. Many people think of the devil as the enemy. However, this is not always the case. We usually think of the devil as the fallen angel, Lucifer or Satan. But, there is this question: Is the devil really an enemy of God? It should be noted that Christ freely went to the desert to be tempted by the devil. In the Book of Job, Satan even went to the Kingdom of God and seemed to have a friendly discussion with God. If the devil is truly an enemy, why would God talk to him like that and even welcome him into the kingdom?

Is the devil really our enemy or mankind? In some Jewish teachings, it is believed that the devil is an important part of God's plan. He is working for God in accordance with His plan for humanity and the whole universe. Still, the majority school of thought is that the devil is the one who is actively seeking people to destroy. This can be found in many Christian writings after the life of Christ.

These days, many people blame the devil for the evils that they themselves willfully create. In fact, due to the evils of humanity these days, it would seem that the devil and all his demons can just take a break, and yet the evils of humanity will still keep growing and growing. This is because humans are now capable of creating evil. Sadly, in this world, it is evident that there is more evil than good.

So, is the devil really our enemy or is he there simply to challenge us so that our souls can evolve? I would leave it to my readers to decide on this matter. You do not need to have an answer right now. I understand that this is something that is difficult to answer with certainty. However, do not let this discussion affect your faith. It may affect your faith in humanity, but it must never affect your faith in Christ. After all, the truth still remains that Christ is real, and that He is the one and only true living God.

Beware of the Devil's Realm

The devil's realm is a realm of false or illusory enlightenment. It is not negative in the sense that your state of mind will be filled with negativity and stress; but on the contrary, it is a positive feeling and would also fill you with positivity. However, what makes this wrong is that it is not the end of the spiritual journey and development. It is the temptation to stop developing and growing. This is usually faced once you gain some maturity and experience in the spiritual life. The devil will want you to think and feel that you have attained what you needed to attain and that you have reached whatever is there that you must accomplish. However, the truth is that you have probably only reached half of the journey, and there is simply so much to be done. But, the devil will do its best to stop you by just making you feel good about yourself.

By this time, the devil knows that he could no longer use the usual temptations that appear evil on its face, so he will resort to more clever ways of preventing you from having an intimate communion with Divinity.

So, how do you overcome the devil's realm? We must understand that we cannot avoid getting into this realm since the devil is the one that will initiate it. But, once we are in this realm through the work of the devil, we can easily protect ourselves.

How do we protect ourselves from the devil's realm? The answer is simple: Go back to the basics of the faith. This means not thinking and worrying about it and simply surrendering everything to God. An important step here is to remain humble. Again, humility is very important as it allows the infinite graces of God to work in and through us.

The key is to keep all of our focus on God and surrender everything to Him. If the devil tries to make us feel good and satisfied with everything, just enjoy the sense of fulfillment but keep all your focus on God. He alone will guide and protect us.

As you can see, it is not what the senses perceive that matters. Our senses can be deluding at times, and they can easily be tricked by the devil. We must not forget that we are not the senses. You have a body, but it is not you. In the same way, we have senses, but we are not the senses. If the senses give us a sense of pleasure and accomplishment, we can enjoy such fleeting pleasures of life, but all of our efforts and focus must be directed on Christ alone. It is not pleasing the senses that matter, but it is pleasing Christ that is important.

Therefore, let us keep our focus on Christ no matter what. Let us not be fooled by transitory feelings. Instead, we should surrender everything to God, and allow Him to have complete control of our lives—for this is the way to living the life of a true Christian mystic.

Beware of the Modern World

We must beware that we are in the territory of the enemy. The system of the world is designed in such a way that one ought to forget about Christ. These days, humans are always bombarded with so many things to do and worry about. The modern world even makes one forget that he is a soul. Indeed, the modern system has many tricks and deception at play. It has now become a common teaching that one must not believe everything that they see on the news and on social media right away. Indeed, this world is full of deceptions. This is also the reason why in the lives of many mystics, they tend to step away from the crowd, away from the world by living a solitary life. As long as you are in this world, you will be facing so much evil because the forces of evil are always at work in this world.

When dealing with the modern world, the practice of meditation, such as the *Jesus Prayer*, would be very helpful. Meditation allows us to declutter the mind. A common trick of this world is to fill the mind with so many things to think and worry about so that one will have no more time to focus on their spiritual growth, and so that you will not have enough time to even focus on Christ. When we are faced with this challenge, we must learn to let go of everything, including all the thoughts that may appear necessary. Instead, we should only fill our hearts and minds with Christ. By doing this, we can be sure that we have the right foundation, and it will also allow for the graces of God to flow and manifest in our lives.

You should also be careful with another trick of this world: false literature. This is where the world preaches a teaching that is no in accordance with the will of God. We can easily know God's will for it is always in harmony with the words and teachings of Christ in the Bible. I know a man who has lost all faith because of doing so much research. Doing research is good, but just make sure that it will help your soul to grow and not the other way around.

It is worth stressing that the system of this world is full of deceptions, so be on your guard. Let us trust in Jesus Christ and not in this world, for this world and the many works thereof are evil. This world is also known for combining lies with the truth. Not only that, but the world will even give you a taste of wisdom. It may sound and appear very reasonable on its face. However, let us remember the words in the sacred scriptures that the wisdom of man is a mere folly before God. After all, our little minds are nothing as compared with the Infinite Mind of the One True God, Jesus Christ. Resounding the words in the Book of Psalms, His ways are always higher than our ways, and His thoughts are always higher than our thoughts. We are only human, and Christ is God. Do you still desire to follow the world or would you rather take a leap of faith and follow the Divine?

Focus on the Action, Not the Fruits

The teaching to focus on the action and not on the fruits of action is actually found in the Hindu scripture, *Bhagavad Gita*. Interestingly, this teaching is also very much applicable to being a Christian mystic. Many of us give too much importance to the fruits or results of our actions. Maybe because we have been exposed to a world where nothing seems to matter but the end result; and that sadly, even if the means to an end is evil, it becomes a common and acceptable practice as long as you get the desired result, such as profit in business or successfully closing a deal, and so on. This approach is very much different from an honest spiritual life. As a follower of Christ, we must not put so much emphasis on the fruits of our actions. In fact, if we truly empty (humble) ourselves, we must not be concerned about the fruits of our actions at all. Following Christ is all that matters, not the fruits of actions.

Another reason why we should not focus on the fruits of actions is that it tends to divide the energy that we have. Instead of putting all our energy to a single point, we become divided when we place emphasis on the fruits. We should understand that the fruits of actions will happen on their own as long as the actions take place. Therefore, a better approach is to put all of our efforts and energy into the actions themselves. In this case, we dedicate all our energy to following Christ. The fruits will arrive on their own. The fruits are the work of God, not ours.

It should also be noted that we do not follow Christ just for the sake of the rewards. If we follow Him just for the sole purpose of being rewarded, then we are not worthy to be His disciple. If the reward is our goal, then we are following the reward and not Christ. Do not worry for now, as you gain more spiritual maturity, you will have the understanding and wisdom on this matter. Still, it is good that you are aware of this as early as now even if only on an intellectual level. Soon enough, as you follow Christ, your soul will grow more and more beautifully, and you will realize everything—and when this happens, you can smile and even shout for joy for following Christ.

Admit that You Do Not Know

You might think of mystics as people who have answers for everything. However, such is a wrong perception of a real mystic. In fact, if you study the lives of many mystics who have lived, you will see that they lived a very simple life with very simple and even child-like character. In our world, people always want to know things and to always have an answer for everything. Many times, even when they do not know or are unsure of something, they still pretend to know. We are just not used to being humble and admitting that we do not know. But, the truth is that the human mind is too inadequate to know the many mysteries of God—and the mysteries of God are only revealed by Him to those who are humble of mind and heart. This is where the mystics go many steps ahead of us—because they are humble, and so God teaches them.

Even if we follow Christ, it does not mean that life will be easy and pleasant to us all the time. Nevertheless, no matter what happens, we can be happy because we know that we are with Him, The Eternal God, Jesus Christ.

We may not have the answers to many things, but Christ has. By being with Him, then we know that we have the answers with us. Nevertheless, it must be clarified that it is not important in spiritual life to have answers to everything. In fact, one thing is necessary, and that is only to follow Jesus. All others are just for entertainment.

As you can see, God is not demanding so much from us. It is humans who are usually the ones demanding too much from another human being. If we read the teachings of Christ, they are also very simple—and they are actually for our own good, not for His own good.

By admitting that we do not know, by acknowledging our nothingness and littleness, we can be a vessel for divine grace. But, if we follow the ways of this world and always keep our cup overflowing, then the graces of the Almighty could not flow through us. Indeed, there is so much power in humility. Socrates is said to be the wisest man. This is so because he told the Oracle, "I know that I do not know." Let us also be humble and admit that we do not know—and Jesus will teach us and lead us to all truth. God is Truth.

Best Practices

Let us now discuss the essential best practices that you can observe to further enhance your experience of being a solitary Christian mystic:

Make time for prayer

Be sure to make time for prayer. In our modern world, it is very easy to get misdirected and be too busy that there is hardly any time to pray. Make your prayer like a priority. You should make a conscious and active effort to make this work. It should also be noted that meditation is also considered as prayer. Be sure to meditate daily. As much as possible, meditate at least twice every day/night.

Always follow the teachings of Christ

The ways of Christ may not always conform to the ways of the world. For example, the world tells us to crush our enemies and show no mercy, but Christ teaches us to love our enemies. The test to know that we are a true disciple of Christ is if we are truly living the words of Christ in our everyday life.

Make Bible-reading a habit

It is highly recommended to read the Bible every day, especially the parts concerning the life and teachings of the Divine Master, Jesus Christ. To experience mystical encounters, apply the Alexandrian method regularly.

Pray the *Jesus Prayer*

The Jesus Prayer is a well-tested prayer, and many saints and holy people have attested to the power of this prayer. Be sure to take advantage of it by praying it as often as you can. It is a simple, direct, and effective technique that can elevate your soul to the Divine. From an occult standpoint, it is also the kind of prayer that will naturally develop your overall spiritual and psychic faculties.

Live a simple life

The life of a mystic can be achieved through a simple life. The modern world will do its best to keep your life very busy and complex, thereby taking away the time that you need to focus on Christ. It is strongly suggested to keep your life as simple as possible. Never allow the things that you do and the things that you possess to own you.

Learn from others

Since you are now pursuing the True Path, it is also good to learn from those who have gone before you. In this regard, we can learn so much from the documented lives of the saints, as well as from the holy people who are still alive. This will allow us to gain wisdom from them, as well as gain inspiration to continue the journey. Personally, I strongly recommend that you watch Father Lazarus. He was an atheist until the age of 40. He now lives in complete solitary in the desert of Egypt as a Christian monk. As of the time of writing, 2022, he is still alive. I consider him as one of the very few living saints in the world. To know more about him, you may access YouTube, and simply key in the search box the following: Fr. Lazarus el Anthony.

Always love

The teachings of Christ can be summarized in one word: love. The way to Christ is a way of love. Little by little, we lose ourselves as we transform into something greater than us: the very soul of love. Loving may not always be easy, but it is something that we can do. After all, Jesus is always with us, so we know that everything is possible — and we can always love, for God is love.

Rely on Jesus

True faith finds its strength in having complete dependence on God. We can always rely on Jesus. In fact, everything that happens in our life relies on God. You may have so many plans with your life; but at any time, God can create changes. All wise people know that we are always dependent on God even if we do not acknowledge it. Having a child-like reliance and dependence on Christ can create wonders in your life. This kind of trust, a form of ultimate reliance, is also the way of the mystics.

Stop thinking logically

One thing that prevents man from experiencing the divine mystery is because of their logical thinking. We fail to understand that human logic incredibly falls short when compared with the wisdom of God. We are like little ants trying to understand chemistry. It may be good to use some logic when dealing with simple matters of the physical world, but when it comes to having a union with God, we must admit that we know nothing and can do nothing. We must surrender ourselves to the Divine, and only then can we taste the sweet mystery of Divinity.

Stop thinking. Your brain will only prevent you from having miraculous and mystical experiences. Trust in Christ, and let go.

Have fun

Enjoy the mystical journey. It is good to serve Christ with a cheerful spirit. Let us stop complaining; and instead, we should start believing and having faith. If we truly realize that we belong to Jesus and that we have surrendered everything in our life in His hands, then there is nothing for us to worry about. We can just be happy and enjoy the adventure that Christ has for us. It is a life with Him and in Him. Having Jesus is always more than enough. Now that you have Christ, be happy, always.

The Author

www.charlzdelacruz.com

Password to enter the private page: ANGEL912

Don't miss out!

Visit the website below and you can sign up to receive emails whenever Gideon Crusader publishes a new book. There's no charge and no obligation.

https://books2read.com/r/B-A-VRRV-IAADC

BOOKS 2 READ

Connecting independent readers to independent writers.

Did you love *The Solitary Christian Mysticism Manual*? Then you should read *Frugal Living for Happiness & Freedom*[1] by Gideon Crusader!

[2]

Frugal Living for Happiness & Freedom is a life manual that will teach you the importance of being frugal, as well as how you can live a happy and fulfilling life while spending very little money. No matter what people may tell you, the truth is that you do not need so much money in your life to be truly happy. In fact, many times, money is what misdirects us and blinds us from the real source of happiness in our life.

---

1. https://books2read.com/u/mZEMKD

2. https://books2read.com/u/mZEMKD

It should be noted that being frugal is not about being cheap. There is a big difference between being frugal and being cheap. You are not cheap. It is just that, when you are frugal, it only shows that you now understand and view money as it really is. It means that you now understand the real worth and value of money — and that now you know that you are not dependent on money for your happiness.

Frugal Living for Happiness & Freedom will give you the right foundation that you need to experience real happiness and freedom by living a frugal life. When you pursue this lifestyle, it is important that you have the right foundation. This foundation is based on your understanding and view as to what living a frugal life really means. In this regard, it is important that you have the right view on what money is really all about. In this book, we will discuss the importance of money and how it relates to happiness and the way of a frugal lifestyle.

Frugal Living for Happiness & Freedom reveals teachings that you can apply into your daily life right now at this very moment. These teachings can create positive changes in your life. But, it is up to you to put the teachings into actual practice and actually make them work in your life. The good news is that it is actually easy to live a frugal lifestyle, and it will also help you achieve true happiness and freedom.

Are you ready to enjoy a frugal lifestyle? Are you ready to have more time in your hands and be happier in your life? If yes, then let me now welcome you into this beautiful world where love, peace of mind, and happiness are more important and valuable than money. This is the way of the true human being. Now is the time for you to actually live your life to the fullest and be who you truly are. Be happy and be free.

Also by Gideon Crusader

Magic Quest
A Codex on Creating a Magical Phantom
Prosperity Magic for Money & Wealth
Telekinesis Bible
Beware of the Modern World
The Solitary Christian Mysticism Manual

Standalone
Frugal Living for Happiness & Freedom